Creative Doodle Games for Trainers, Coaches, Facilitators - Fun Games for Serious Business

doodlevision

Creative Doodle Games for Trainers, Coaches, Facilitators - Fun Games for Serious Business

Forget the Box Doodle-Based Activities for Business and Multi-Language Working Groups

LISA ROSE

authorHOUSE®

AuthorHouse™ UK Ltd.
1663 Liberty Drive
Bloomington, IN 47403 USA
www.authorhouse.co.uk
Phone: 0800.197.4150

Published by AuthorHouse 12/18/2013

ISBN: 978-1-4918-8476-8 (sc)
ISBN: 978-1-4918-8477-5 (e)

Contents

Acknowledgements vii

About the Author...ix

Introduction...1

Guidelines for Choosing the doodlevision Games and Exercises:......................5

Facilitator To-Doodle Dos!..6

A Quick Word of Advice for Conducting
Doodle-based Training, Workshops or Meetings 8

Ice-Breakers & Energizers—Group Building & Focusing 11

Who doodled? 13

Doodle Doing 15

What Do You Want Out of This Workshop or Meeting?...............................16

What I like About You – Street Artist Style 18

What's on Your Mind? 20

If We Were 22

Will the Real Mr./Ms. Smith Please Stand Up? 24

United States State Mottos 26

Leadership.. 29

Doodling Character Traits of Great Leaders...31

Doodle Thinking - Great Leaders & their Vision 33

What's in My Toolbox? 36

Leadership Styles 38

Heavy is the head that Wears the Crown 40

Cartoon Experience...42

Customer Service, Relationships & Communication 45

Customer Solar Systems 47
All Together Us 49
Dealing with Difficult Customers 51
ABCs of Customer Service and Sales Strategies 53
Inventing Sales Machines 55

Strategic Vision: Corporate Processes, New Products, & Market Development 57

Snakes & Ladders 59
Castaways 61
Stereotypes for Strategy 63
Playing Cards – Product or Market Development 65

Corporate Culture & Business Overviews 71

Multiple Destinations 73
Conquistador or Colonist 75
What Are We? 77
The Devil You Know 79
Transformers 81

Appendices 83

A bit of Trainer Banter for "selling the idea of doodling" to your company, a client or during trainings & meetings 85
Doodling for Health 89
Some Famous Compulsive Doodlers: 91
The Doodle Down the Ages 93
Some Random Doodle Thoughts 95
doodlevision Business and Group Services 98
Why not Consider doodlevision 100

Acknowledgements

Any project such as this is a team effort. There is no way I could possibly thank all the people I have been fortunate to work with; I have learned equally from clients and colleagues in my training and coaching and look forward to continuing to learn more!

The material in this book adjusts and doodle-fies games and exercises that have been used by trainers for many years and games that I have created to meet specific client needs.

The exercises in this book have come from all sources and no sources in particular and I believe their strength is in the creative processes and evolutions that all doodling can allow. It is my hope that the doodlevision materials in this book will offer you a new way to look at your existing methods and materials as well.

I believe that introducing the idea of doodling benefits your work in many more ways than just through the use of these materials, it can benefit you in the way you work, design and plan your own sessions.

I am hoping to see a doodlefication of the Business and Community Nation!

About the Author

For nearly 20 years I have been designing and running workshops, meetings and seminars from Budapest to Belfast. My love of doodling was initially sparked as a means to cross cultural and language barriers and the need to convey complicated concepts in a clear way for non-native English speakers. Through these doodling experiences I realized that that the multi-cultural groups grasped complicated concepts and situations more creatively and more concretely than my standard native English-speaking clients.

Gradually, I realized that greater clarity and creativity can be found in all subjects and with native and non-native English speakers and I began to work with doodling more and more. I now incorporate doodling in all of my work—I doodle in meetings, when designing sessions and even use it as a form of quiet meditation to unwind after a challenging day.

Introduction

Using doodlevision's interactive, visual and kinetic working methods, serious challenges will be faced in new ways and previously unseen solutions and directions will be discovered.

If you're reading this book, you probably already know that humor and innovative engagement can bring new life, commitment and energy to groups that are losing their steam. Everyone can remember from childhood the fun in creating visual representations of their thoughts and ideas; when we were young we were all experts at this way of "seeing" the world and things around us. For most of us, as we got older we were trained to see things more verbally and, as a result, our vision of situations has become more narrow. Words are limited after all, but by engaging your group in more visual activities through directed (and non-directed) doodling, a whole new perspective can be gained.

The method allows for fun and humor to be put back into situations to create possibilities that may have previously been unrecognized or unanticipated.

Why Doodling Does the Trick

The VARK Model of Learning defines 4 methods in which people learn, they are:

Visual (drawing/seeing)
Auditory (voice/hearing)
Reading and Writing (written word)
Kinesthetic (movement/doing)

Traditional Western education and business is heavily focused on the reading and writing methods of learning. Quite naturally, our way of learning in formal education is translated by us to the business word. I would argue, however, that on some level we are still drawn to the power of the visual in the business world even if we're not comfortable with it– take MS PowerPoint for example. The power in making the point is a toe-dipping into the visual for people who are still living within the "only words make you credible" walls.

For many business people, the written word is safe, permanent, feels concise and we're comfortable with it because of our life-long conditioning that it is the primary way to communicate "serious" information and ideas. The written word in business is sometimes appropriately restrictive; it is a necessary part of business life that there are standard formats for communication and contracts. However, in the corporate world, the other areas of understanding information have been neglected. I would argue that this neglect leads to less productivity, creativity and possibility.

Movements, sound and seeing are inherently creative methods of communication, they offer possibilities of understanding things differently, change becomes more fluid and easy to consider. This method of understanding offers not only the people who are viewing a visual representation the opportunity to understand a situation more clearly (or even differently, doodles can be obscure and ambiguous and lend themselves to a variety of interpretations), it also offers the person creating the doodle to see things in a different light when doodling.

The doodling games and exercises in this book combine all four of VARK's learning styles: movement, sound, seeing and the written word, so you see, doodling, while fun, is actually a serious business!

This book can offer you and your group the opportunity to consider and explore new possibilities, weigh out options and plan forward in ways that traditional meetings and workshops simply cannot do!

How to Use This Book

There are 28 doodlevision exercises in this book. They are designed to be included as exercises in workshops and meetings that are more traditionally run (some of them can easily be added in as activities in the day's agenda) as well as used in workshops or meetings that will use doodling for the entire meeting's agenda.

Each game or exercise lists the instructions in the same format:

Objectives
Materials Required
Procedure
Tips and Discussion Questions

I've kept the timings to the bare minimum for the exercises; if you've more time, take it, I have also noted variations on the methods under Tips and Discussions.

I encourage anyone planning a doodlevision session to read the appendices of this book, they will help you to understand doodling and offer you some fun facts, trivia and scientific back up to the benefits of using doodling in our business and personal lives.

Guidelines for Choosing the doodlevision Games and Exercises:

1. Be sure that the game or exercise you choose supports the topic that you will be discussing (don't just choose one because it sounds like so much fun!).
2. Make certain that the game or exercise you choose can be done in the space of time you have available.
3. Be sure you are clear on how to play, lead and facilitate the exercise you have chosen.
4. Doodle in the book! Next to exercises try out some of the doodling of concepts or instructions – see what you come up with – it will help you when you run the workshops and also may lead you down some new ways of using or modifying them to suit your needs or individual style.
5. Practice the exercise before you actually use it with your first group.
6. Ask yourself if the game or exercise clearly fits with your previously defined specific objectives for the meeting, storming or workshop.
7. Modify or tailor your exercise to suit your audiences' needs.
8. Try to second-guess where the glitches may happen (by knowing the personalities (if possible) and any inherent limitations (environment, time and group size).
9. Build in some flexibility! Since doodlevision is all about pulling out untapped creativity and perspectives, prepare to be surprised! Know ahead of time what steps or bits you can be flexible with so that if something the group wants to explore comes up you can take a good look at it (or schedule another session).

Facilitator To-Doodle Dos!

Here's a simple Checklist to use when you're preparing, conducting, closing and evaluating a session (if you're doing more than one exercise just repeat the first "box"):

To-do	How To-Do/What to Take	Done
Exercise Knowledge	Practice the Exercise (in your head or on some friends!)	_____
	Gather All Materials Needed (each section gives a full list). Here's a space to fill:	_____
	_____	
	_____	
	_____	
	_____	
	_____	
	_____	
Times Set for the Day (considering breaks/ lunch etc.)		_____

Checking the Rhythm	At the breaks, take a quick look at your timings and see if there is anything you need to adjust, ask yourself:	_____
	Based on the pace of the first session, are your timings right? Groups work at different paces and have their own personalities. Some get too wrapped up in the fun; make sure you are still heading in the right direction with the core purpose. Make adjustments if you need to.	_____
	Is there anyone "just not getting it" and, if not, why? What can you do?	_____
	Do you need to either focus them more or loosen them up a bit? Try one of the folly exercises.	_____
Evaluation Forms	Design Evaluation Forms which offer the opportunity for your group to include doodling in their response!	_____
Self-Session Review	Before you look at the evaluations by the participants, take 5 minutes and write down your observations—what worked, what didn't? Is there anything that you would add to or would like to take more time to explore next time?	_____
Gather up the Doodles!	If you are conducting sessions for your own company keep them in a file—they can be great ways to start new sessions, remind people of their visions and spark new ideas ahead (you can use them to focus the group if there are any follow up sessions planned—just put them around the room and let the group reminisce when they arrive for the next session), a great way to get them back on track without formally getting them back on track! Or, if any are particularly relevant or brilliant and you'd like to get them out to show other employees, set up an impromptu gallery of the works in the staff kitchen or lobby (with doodler's permission of course).	_____

A Quick Word of Advice for Conducting Doodle-based Training, Workshops or Meetings

When introducing doodling to a new group, make sure you keep the time icebreakers or energizers tight for the doodling. Also remind them that they can use the odd word or phrase in their doodles—make sure they understand that doodling is not an anti-word medium.

You will have some in the group who are not comfortable doodling (who may feel like they do not have the skills or aren't "good enough"). To help offset this, for the icebreakers try to make the time quick for the drawing (you may even decide 5 minutes for some of the exercises is too long) so the people who are naturally comfortable with their artistic talents won't have time to produce something that looks like Rembrandt (depending on the personalities in the room, some could find that intimidating!). The time pressure will help make the unnatural doodlers more comfortable and the super-duper doodlers less competitive.

People can also often be quite competitive when they first start these sorts of sessions; I've found that once you get through the first one, the group understands that it's not about doodling the best technically, it's about creativity. This will be understood by all in the room once you've gotten things rolling.

If a lesson plan mentions putting the doodles on the wall, if you've space please do, it allows for referral throughout the session or meeting and can spark some ideas that in traditional meeting/workshop formats can sometimes get lost or be forgotten. If you can put them on the wall, encourage people throughout the day to doodle away on them – they may want to add bits as they pop up – being encouraged to return to the doodles will also help them to continue to explore the ideas that pop up as they appear.

Doodling is about achieving clarity of thought and some of the exercises in this book are mini-doodle meditations and are not seeking representation, they are more about contemplation.

If a session plan doesn't call for specific representations remind the participants that it's okay for the doodles to be totally abstract or random, it is up to the doodler to then talk about what they were thinking about as they doodled.

Finally, when group doodling is required – make certain that the group know it is a COLLABORATIVE doodle – everyone should have a pen in hand and everyone should be helping to address the issue/task given. It is not about one member "doing" the flipchart for the group (which is what people are used to and comfortable with). Make certain you work the room during group sessions and that everyone has a pen in hand and is doodling!

The Most Important Thing!

Stress to everyone that all doodlevision exercises are about widening our vision, gaining new perspectives and seeing things in ways that language alone cannot convey—it is not about being fantastic artists. Doodling is about creative, spontaneous ways of getting a message across without the worry of being technically correct, proportionate or perfect.

Ice-Breakers & Energizers—
Group Building & Focusing

Who doodled?

10 - 15 Minutes

Objective:
To get the group to relax about the medium of doodling and allow them to think about doodling as a credible and creative way for people to assist themselves to think, problem solve, listen or absorb information. There are an awful lot of famous and successful doodlers out there!

Materials Required
A PowerPoint (if you find your own be sure to note sources and follow copyright, you can find them easily on the internet)

Procedure
Show PowerPoint slides or pass around A4 print outs of famous doodles. You can find a list of famous doodlers in the appendix, visit my website (www. doodlevisionltd.com - fun facts page) or search on the Internet for doodles that will suit your group best. You will be spoiled for choice.

Show the doodles and ask, with each one, who they think might have been the doodler—if they can't guess who (some of them can be quite challenging) have them guess for a while before you tell them the answers.

Tips and Discussion Points
During or before the game, tell the group some of the information that can be found in the appendix of this book—they will be interested to hear both the fun and factual materials.

Ask them if they were surprised by the wide variety of people who doodled. Try to mix up your doodlers to include mathematicians, politicians, poets, businessmen and scientists. It will help to demonstrate that people from all walks of life doodle.

Once you have completed your series, the group will have discovered for themselves that some great minds doodle and the rest of the workshop or meeting will have developed an underlying "respect" for the medium of doodling!

Doodle Doing

10 minutes for the doodling
5 - 10 minutes for the doodle gallery

Objectives:
To get the group to accept and become comfortable with doodling.

Materials Required:
Pens
Distribute the printed agenda to the group. 2 copies for each person.
Post-it notes
Blu Tack

Procedure:
Hand out one copy each of the agenda.

Ask them to doodle as you talk them through the plans for the session.

Try to talk a little more than necessary. You could tell them interesting facts about doodling (see appendix) or just stick to the business of the session.

Gather the doodled agendas once you're done with the introduction.

Pass out the other copies of the agenda (one each).

Tell them they will see them later on.

Gather the agendas from the group.

When they are on their first coffee/tea break put the doodled agendas up on the wall and ask them who did which doodle.

Tips or Discussion Points:
How many did they get right?

Why did they know who did which doodle; what tipped them off?

Where they surprised by what anyone doodled?

What Do You Want Out of This Workshop or Meeting?

5 minutes for the doodling
10 minutes for the Interactions/Viewing

Objectives:
To get the group to doodle their expectations of the meeting or workshop.

Materials Required:
Pens
1 Sheet of A4 paper
Blu Tack

Procedure:
Hand out one sheet of paper and pens

Ask them to doodle the most important thing they want to walk away with at the end of the session. In the exercise, the doodling can include the odd word or phrase, but encourage them to think about how they can represent what they want visually.

Hand out some Blu Tack to each participant and ask him or her to put their doodles on the wall and allow the group to wander around and see what others are expecting. If they find agreements in expectations, ask them to put a check mark (or better still, a representative doodle) on the relevant sheet. Encourage them to explain their doodles to each other.

This will give you a clear picture of expectations as well and help to ensure that the perceived most important aspects of the workshop or meeting are delivered.

Tips or Discussion Points:

This will give you a clear picture of expectations as well and help to ensure that the perceived most important aspects of the workshop or meeting are delivered or tabled to address at the next one!

What I like About You – Street Artist Style

10 minutes for the doodling
1 - 2 minutes for each interpretation/presentation

Objectives:
To get the group doodling and, particularly if it is going to be a challenging session, to remind the team of the aspects of their co-workers that are positive or that they appreciate.

Materials Required:
Pens—you can provide only one color pen or offer the group choices of colors
Blank A4 paper, a sheet for each participant
Clipboards one for each participant
Blu Tack

Procedure:
Hand out one blank sheet, clipboard and pen per participant.

Randomly match them in pairs (if numbers aren't even, make one a trio), or if you know of any people who work together and may be having difficulties, if you feel it's a good idea and you're capable for the situation, match the pairs purposely.

Ask them to create either a caricature, Pablo Picasso style, impressionistic style, whatever style strikes their fancy to represent what they appreciate the other person does for them in the workplace, can do or any other complimentary thing about them that they can represent.

Sit them opposite one another, as you would see a caricaturist working on a city sidewalk. Ask them to doodle their pieces at the same time; they can even have a bit of banter while they do. Ask them to write the name of the person they have drawn on the sheet as well.

When you've called time on the "street art" part of this session, pull the group back together and ask them to exchange the posters with a different person in the group.

Then ask each person to get up and present the work of art about another member and explain the meaning of the doodle.

Tips or Discussion Points:

Make sure you keep to the positives—it should be a bit of light-hearted fun and banter!

What's on Your Mind?

5 minutes to draw
10 minutes to view

Objectives:
To get the group doodling and thinking about what concerns them the most about a topic or issue (not what they are expecting to get out of it).

Materials Required:
Pens – you can provide only one color pen or offer the group choices of colors
Blank A4 paper, a sheet for each participant
Blu Tack

Procedure:
Hand out one blank sheet and ask them a question designed to focus them on them issues to be addressed for the meeting or workshop—the question can be positive or negative (some sample questions are listed below to kick-start you) but make sure they are relevant to the topic for the day.

Tips or Discussion Points:
This works particularly well when you're dealing with a group that is feeling negative or there's some friction. By using doodling people will be more open to expression as this method of communicating can seem less threatening—the message can get across without the need for too much explaining!

Some suggested questions are:

What are you most concerned about with this topic/discussion?

What worries you the most in dealing with this situation?

What do you think are the most valuable assets/sales points/skills concerning today's discussions?

What are the best perspectives or skills that you bring to today's topic or workshop?

Tailor the question to the group's agenda as much as you can; it's not about what they expect to walk away with, it's about what they feel they are coming in with—the challenges and the contribution.

If We Were . . .

10 minutes to draw
15 - 20 Minutes to Present

Objectives:
To get the group doodling and thinking what the corporate "personality" is or what type of challenge is being faced in the workshop or meeting.

Materials Required:
Pens – A variety of colors, enough for each group of participants
Flip Chart Paper
Blu Tack

Procedure:
Divide the group into working groups of 3 or more. Ask them one of the suggested questions in "Tips or Discussions"—whichever one you feel will be most accessible (or challenging!) for the group or, if you'd like to, make up one of your own.

Have the groups come back together after 10 minutes to briefly explain their doodle to the larger group.

Tips or Discussion Points:
Some suggested questions are:

If our organization (or the issue we are addressing in the workshop or meeting) were a tree, what type would it be?

If our organization (or the issue we are addressing in the workshop or meeting) were a person, what would they look like?

If our organization (or the issue we are addressing the workshop or meeting) were an island, what would it look like?

If our organization (or the issue we are addressing in the workplace or meeting) were the weather, what is the weather forecast for yesterday, today and tomorrow?

Be creative—there are many, many options for comparison. You could try to come up with something that compares with the industry or sector of the group.

Tailor the question to the group's agenda as much as you can—it's not about what they expect to walk away with, it's about what they feel they are coming in with, the challenges and the contribution.

Will the Real Mr./Ms. Smith Please Stand Up?

5 minutes for the drawing
1 - 2 minutes per card introduction

Objectives:
To break the ice by getting the group to introduce themselves through their doodles.

Materials Required:
Pens – you can provide only one color pen or offer the group choices of colors
Blank Note Cards (3 x 5)

Procedure:
Hand out one blank card for each person and pen(s).

Ask them to doodle something about themselves on the cards; they can doodle anything they'd like—their hobbies, something about their job, interests or families—anything that can describe them is acceptable. They are to write their names on the other side of the card (not on the doodle side). Allow only 5 minutes for this.

Collect the cards and shuffle them (like they were playing cards, with picture side up/in view) and then, one at a time, ask each person to come to the front of the room and select a card from the shuffle (picture side up). The introducer is only allowed to look at the doodle side while holding the name side of the card out to face the audience.

The introducer then tells the group as much as possible about the card owner by only interpreting the doodles; they can make assumptions or inferences as desired. The introduction should take 1 minute each (it will help make the introducer comfortable, not feeling like they have to stretch out their interpretation).

After each "introduction" the person who drew the doodle joins the introducer and can clarify, correct or add anything they would like to their introduction and doodle interpretation.

Repeat the process until all the cards are drawn.

Tips or Discussion Points:

If you think people in the group are a bit shy about the exercise, take the first card and make the first introduction.

United States State Mottos

10 minutes for the flags
1 - 2 minutes for each presentation of the flags

Objectives:
To break the ice and help the group to focus on the organization's goals or meeting/ workshop's purpose.

Materials Required:
Pens – Enough colors for each paired group to have a variety
Pre-Prepared Note Cards (3 x 5)
Flip Chart Paper with the same sized flag outline pre-drawn.
Blu Tack

Procedure:
Hand out one pre-prepared card for each person (see Tips and Discussion Points) and pen(s).

Pair the group in whatever way you feel appropriate (either randomly or purposefully).

Tell them that each pair is holding a state motto and their task is to use the motto to focus and apply it to the organization or workshop/meeting topic. To represent how it applies they need to draw a flag that will reflect how it has meaning with respect to the organization, workshop or meeting.

Give them only 10 minutes for the task and then ask them to present their work to the group (1-2 minutes each)

Put the flags around the room for the duration of the workshop or meeting.

Tips or Discussion Points:

My top 10 state mottos for this workshop are:

Regnat Populus (The People Rule), Arkansas

Eureka (I have found it), California

Ad Astra Per Aspera (To the stars through difficulties), Kansas

Crescit Eundo (It grows as it goes), New Mexico

Esse Quam Videri (To be, rather than to seem), North Carolina

Lavor Omnia Vincit (Labor conquers all things), Oklahoma

Alis Volat Propriis (She flies with her own wings), Oregon

Dum Spiro Spero, Animis Opibusque Parati (While I breathe, I hope. Ready in soul and resource), South Carolina

Excelsior (Ever Upwards), New York

Leadership

Doodling Character Traits of Great Leaders

5 minutes for doodling
1 - 2 minutes for each discussion
5 minutes for people to add to each other's doodles

Objectives:
To focus the group on what makes a "Great Leader" using 14 characteristics

Materials Required:
Pens – Enough colors for each paired group to have a variety
Flipchart Paper (1 for each pair)
Blu Tack

Procedure:
Pair the group in whatever way you feel appropriate (either randomly or purposefully). If you've an odd number, one group can be 3.

Give each pair one of the 14 traits of a great leader and ask them to doodle what the traits mean to them—they can doodle anything (a person, where the character traits "come from", what makes up the trait . . . anything they'd like).

Give them only 5 minutes for the task and then ask them to present their work to the group (1-2 minutes each)

Once a presentation is finished, have the pair put the flipchart on the wall in the room.

When the whole group is finished with their presentations, ask them to walk around the room and add to the existing doodles, whatever they think should also be included.

Tips or Discussion Points:
14 Leadership Character Traits
Integrity

Knowledge

Courage

Decisiveness

Dependability

Initiative

Tact

Justice

Enthusiasm

Bearing

Endurance

Unselfishness

Loyalty

Judgment

Doodle Thinking - Great Leaders & their Vision

10 minutes for doodling
1 - 2 minutes for presentations

Objectives:

To focus the group on what makes a "Great Leader" using quotes from some of the world's greatest leaders.

Materials Required:

Pens – Enough colors for each paired group to have a variety
A sheet, Post-it note or index card with one of the quotes listed in "Tips or Discussion Points"
Flipchart Paper (1 for each pair)
Blu Tack

Procedure:

Pair the group in whatever way you feel appropriate (either randomly or purposefully). If you've an odd number, one group can be 3.

Give each pair one of the quotes listed below (or find some that you'd like to see included) and ask them to doodle what the traits of that person were. They can doodle anything to represent what the person did or, if they don't know much about them (I've found that once they start thinking about it they usually know more than they thought), they can doodle what the quote represents.

Give them only 5 minutes for the task and then ask them to present their work to the group (1-2 minutes each).

Once a presentation is finished, have the pair put the flipchart on the wall in the room.

Tips or Discussion Points:
Quotes:

The best executive is the one who has sense enough to pick good men to do what he wants done, and self-restraint to keep from meddling with them while they do it. Theodore Roosevelt

A leader is a dealer in hope. Napoleon Bonaparte

The ultimate measure of a man is not where he stands in moments of comfort, but where he stands at times of challenge and controversy. Winston Churchill

Innovation distinguishes between a leader and a follower. Steve Jobs

Men make history and not the other way around. In periods where there is no leadership, society stands still. Progress occurs when courageous, skillful leaders seize the opportunity to change things for the better. Harry S. Truman

Great leaders are almost always great simplifiers, who can cut through argument, debate, and doubt to offer a solution everybody can understand. General Colin Powell

It is better to lead from behind and to put others in front, especially when you celebrate victory when nice things occur. You take the front line when there is danger. Then people will appreciate your leadership. Nelson Mandela

The price of greatness is responsibility. Winston Churchill

If you want to build a ship, don't drum up people together to collect wood and don't assign them tasks and work, but rather teach them to long for the endless immensity of the sea. Antoine de Saint-Exupery

As we look ahead into the next century, leaders will be those who empower others. Bill Gates

If time allows, before the pair doodling begins, allow 2 - 3 minutes for each person to doodle on a sheet of paper on their own before they collaborate.

What's in My Toolbox?

5 - 10 minutes for doodling
1 - 2 minutes for each discussion

Objectives:
To allow space for individuals to conduct a self-audit of their skills and leadership qualities.

Materials Required:
Pens – Enough colors for each person to have a variety
Flipchart Paper (1 for each person)
Blu Tack

Procedure:
Start the session with the following quote:
"If the only tool you have is a hammer, you will see every problem as a nail."
Abraham Maslow

Ask the group to think about how many skills and leadership qualities (or tools) they have in their toolbox and to doodle the tools that represent the skills that they bring to leadership in their lives and work.

Have each individual give a quick presentation of the skills and leadership qualities that they can offer others.

Once a presentation is finished, have the person put up the flipchart on the wall in the room (make sure their name is on it).

Tips or Discussion Points:
If you feel the group is right for it, when the whole group is finished with their presentations ask them to walk around the room and add to other people's existing

doodles, whatever they think the person missed about themselves or what should also be included.

You could ask them which tool they use the most and if there is one that is favored, is it always the best one for the job?

This audit can be used to refer to later on in the day as you move through other work or exercises—it's a ready-made skills audit of the group.

Leadership Styles

5 - 10 Minutes
1 - 2 minutes for each discussion

Objectives:
To allow space for individuals to examine various leadership styles and to self-reflect on their own style and that of others around them.

Materials Required:
Pens – Enough colors for each pair to have a variety
Flipchart Paper (1 for each pair)
Blu Tack

Procedure:
Pair the group in whatever way you feel appropriate (either randomly or purposefully). If you've an odd number, one group can be 3.

Explain to the group that Kurt Lewin classified management styles and cultures into three categories—autocratic, democratic and laissez-faire. Give the pairs one of the leadership styles to doodle; they are to represent what the style "looks like", how they interact with others and anything else that occurs to them around the style of leadership.

Have each pair give a quick presentation of the skills and leadership qualities that they can offer others.

Once a presentation is finished, have the person put up the flipchart on the wall in the room (make sure their name is on it).

Tips or Discussion Points:

Ask the group which style they see most in their day-to-day work.

Which style do they think works best?

Perhaps they feel different styles work best in different situations—which ones?

> If time allows, before the group doodling begins, allow 2 - 3 minutes for each person to doodle on a sheet of paper on their own before they collaborate.

Heavy is the head that Wears the Crown

5 - 10 minutes for doodling
1 - 2 minutes for each discussion

Objectives:

To allow space for individuals to conduct a self-audit of their skills and leadership qualities.

Materials Required:

Pens – Enough colors for each person to have a variety
An A4 sheet of paper that has an outline of a crown on it.
Blu Tack

Procedure:

Open the session with the following quote:

"Canst thou, O partial sleep, give thy repose To the wet sea-boy in an hour so rude, And in the calmest and most stillest night, With all appliances and means to boot, Deny it to a king? Then happy low, lie down! Uneasy lies the head that wears a crown." King Henry the Fourth, Part 2, Act 3, scene 1, 26-31

Discuss what the quote means to the group.

Tell them that they are going to think about what "jewels" of leadership are worn by great leaders and ask them to design a crown which represents the qualities of a great leader. Alternatively, ask them to self-reflect and design a crown that represents their leadership qualities.

Have each individual give a quick presentation of their work. Put the crowns up on the wall for the duration of the session. If they are self-representations, ask that they include their names on the doodles.

Tips or Discussion Points:

Some people may want to create their own crown—perfectly ok! You can suggest it to everyone or, if someone asks, make sure everyone in the group knows it's an option.

Cartoon Experience

5 - 10 minutes for doodling
1 - 2 minutes for each discussion

Objectives:
To allow space for individuals to conduct a self-audit of a time when their leadership skills were required

Materials Required:
Pens – Enough colors for each person to have a variety
An A4 sheet of paper
Blu Tack
Scenario (either on flipchart, PowerPoint, or one sheet each for participants)

Procedure:
Introduce the session by stating that we have all had times in our lives when our leadership has been put to the test.

Ask them to do a one-scene doodle that represents a personal experience based on the stated scenario.

Have each individual give a quick presentation of their work. Put the works up on 45 the wall for the duration of the session.

Tips or Discussion Points:
You can give the group different scenarios or have them all do the same one. Below are 3 to choose from (of course, add more if you have any that you'd like to explore!)

Demonstrate a time when you had to work with a team who differed in opinion, approach and objective—how did you create agreement and shared purpose?

Leading in an organization often requires that you build support for your goals and projects from people over whom you have no authority. What did you do in the situation to build the needed support?

Choosing one of your greatest successes, what did the team look like? What were the elements that were successfully brought together?

Customer Service, Relationships & Communication

Customer Solar Systems

15 minutes for doodling
2 - 3 Minutes for Presentations

Objectives:
This exercise is designed to get a customer service team to think about who their clients are, what motivates them, what the threats are to their good relations/ service and how they can better serve client needs.

Materials Required:
Pens – Enough colors for each team to have a variety
Flipchart paper for each participant
Blu Tack

Procedure:
Split the group into groups of 3 - 4 participants.

Explain that their company is like the sun in a solar system. The major clients (or client categories) circle the company sun. Ask them to drawn the solar system identifying the customers/customer sectors as planets that orbit the sun.

Once the teams are ready, have them present their constellations and open the floor to brief discussion about each if appropriate.

Tips or Discussion Points:
If the groups need a bit of a nudge, explain to them that:
The planets' size and distance from the sun can be indicators of importance (or anything else they'd like to interpret).

The orbit trails (drawn circles showing the each planet's trajectory) can represent client motivations (they can draw or write words on the trails).

The sun's rays can represent the solutions, products or services that the company offers each particular planet (or all of them).

Asteroid fields or other representations can demonstrate potential threats to their customer relationships.

Rocket ships or alien ships can also demonstrate services/product or threats.

All Together Us

5 - 10 Minutes for Doodling
2 - 3 Minutes per Team to Present

Objectives:
This exercise is designed to get a customer service team to think about what strengths each of them brings—this can be personal qualities, accounts or any skills that help source and keep customers.

Materials Required:
Pens – Enough colors for each team to have a variety
Flipchart paper for each group
Blu Tack

Procedure:
Break the groups out into groups of 3-4 participants (or larger if appropriate).

Explain that they are going to make a composite person to represent their sales team—the finished doodle could be compared to something like a benevolent "Frankenstein".

When they are finished, ask each group to present and then put the doodles on the wall for the remainder of the session or meeting.

Tips or Discussion Points:
If the groups need a bit of a nudge, explain to them that:

Each member of the team brings something—one may be the best strategic thinker (could be the head of the Customer Team body), one may build the most personal relationships with clients, another may be the most skilled at problem solving (hands perhaps), another might be the fastest responder (feet). Try not to feed all of those listed—too much will mean that they just feedback your suggestions and slot in!

If time allows, before the group doodling begins, allow 2 - 3 minutes for each person to think about their strengths/talents and doodle on a sheet of paper on their own before they collaborate.

Dealing with Difficult Customers

5 - 10 Minutes for 1ˢᵗ Doodling Session
2 - 3 Minutes per Team to Present 1ˢᵗ Doodle
5 - 10 Minutes for 2ⁿᵈ Doodling Session
2 - 3 Minutes to Present

Objectives:

This exercise is designed to get a customer service team to examine any difficult clients and to identify strategies for meeting these clients' needs.

Materials Required:

Pens – Enough colors for each team to have a variety
Flipchart paper for each group
Blu Tack

Procedure:

Break the group into groups of 2 - 3 participants (or larger if appropriate).

Explain to them that they are going to doodle a representation of a difficult customer that they are dealing with or have dealt with—they are only representing the challenges or experiences that this client company or individual is presenting.

Once the 1ˢᵗ doodle session is closed, as the groups to present their doodles.

After each group has presented, exchange the doodles between teams (no team should keep its original doodle).

Put them back in their groups and ask them to doodle solutions or ways to assist the client company or customer to engage more positively so that they can be served better.

Have each group present its Doodle solutions to the whole group. Allow a bit of time for suggestions from the group to add to the solutions and handling of each difficult client/customer.

Put the flipcharts on the wall for the rest of the session/meeting.

Tips or Discussion Points:
You can either have them develop their own characters/representations or give them some of the following stereotypical types of difficult customers/clients to represent:
Leave me Alone Alice
Cut the Price Pat
Know It All Nancy
Suspicious Sam
Dishonest Dan
Impatient Imogene
Argumentative Andy
Moody Mark
Complaining Chris
Bully Boy Bobby
Late Payment Patricia

ABCs of Customer Service and Sales Strategies

5 - 10 Minutes for Doodling
2 - 3 Minutes per Team to Present

Objectives:
This exercise is designed to get a customer service team to think about what strengths each of them brings—this can be personal qualities, accounts or any skills that help source and keep customers.

Materials Required:
Pens – Enough colors for each team or individual (depends on group size) to have a variety
Flipchart paper for each group or individual
Blu Tack

Procedure:
Break the groups into appropriate group sizes or leave as individuals.

Explain that they are going use the alphabet to doodle ideas for customer service and sales strategies for their team.

Assign each person or group 3 alphabet letters each (except for YZ) to doodle on their flipchart. They can take each letter individually (though you will find some combine the three letters into a phrase).

When they are finished, ask each group or individual to present, allow discussion if appropriate and then put the doodles on the wall for the remainder of the session or meeting.

Tips or Discussion Points:

Alphabet Division:

ABC

DEF

GHI

JKL

MNO

PQR

STU

VWX

YZ

Inventing Sales Machines

15 - 20 Minutes for Doodling
2 - 3 Minutes per Team to Present

Objectives:
This exercise is designed to get sales teams to think about the sales process clearly and come up with ways to creatively engage more customers or increase existing sales.

Materials Required:
Pens – Enough colors for each team or individual (depends on group size) to have a variety
Flipchart paper for each group or individual
Blu Tack

Procedure:
Break the groups out into appropriate group sizes or leave as individuals.

Explain that they are going create a machine or invention that will represent the following key areas of creating a successful sales strategy plan:
Pre-Sales Activities Planning (identifying/picking out your targets)
Planning to Execute the Sale (what do you need to make the sale successful?)
Meeting with or contacting the client (what will that look like?)
Delivering the "goods"
Post-Sales Analysis

Once you bring the groups back together allow 2 - 3 minutes for presentation and discussion per group/individual.

Put the doodles on the wall for the remainder of the session or meeting.

Tips or Discussion Points:

I really enjoy this one, but sometimes it takes a bit of teasing out. Some groups have given very "Ford" Factory representations (the process is represented in the manufacturing of a car) of the process, while others have created something more like a Willy Wonka Factory! Once they get into it, it can be a great way to get them to think clearly about a specific sales process or increasing sales with an existing client.

If you feel that giving each group all stages in the process is too time consuming— break them into groups and give each group one step in the process to doodle, then place them in order on the wall. Don't worry if the styles or concepts don't match; it's the content of each step that matters most.

Strategic Vision: Corporate Processes, New Products, & Market Development

Snakes & Ladders

20 - 30 Minutes for Doodling
3 - 5 Minutes per Team to Present

Objectives:
This exercise is designed to get the group to think strategically in a step-by-step process about the development of a corporate direction, new product or specific market development.

Materials Required:
Pens – Enough colors for each team or individual (depends on group size) to have a variety
Flipchart paper for each group or individual
Blu Tack

Procedure:
Break the groups out into appropriate group sizes (a minimum of 3 per group).

Explain that they are going create a new version of Snakes and Ladders. They are tasked with plotting out the topic that is being explored in a step-by-step process (each square of the snake defines one of the processes—encourage them to use visuals/doodles as well as words in the squares (they tend to lean towards words in this game).

Where potential pitfalls are appropriately linked to one of the boxes (or steps in the process), they are to put a snakehead and lead the tail back to where they think the potential setback will take them. Conversely, when they've come up with something in the process that if it works, it will REALLY work, they are to draw a ladder to take them to the place that the success could take them (they will skip some other steps).

Lisa Rose

Once you bring the groups back together, allow 3 - 5 minutes for presentation and discussion per group.

Put the doodles on the wall for the remainder of the session or meeting.

Tips or Discussion Points:
Below is a sample doodle of a blank snakes and ladder for this sort of session. If you feel it appropriate, give this to the teams drawn on a flipchart already for them to doodle in—DON'T include the ladders or snakes as you will not be able to anticipate that part of the process, have them draw their own.

Castaways

30 - 35 Minutes for Doodling
3 - 5 Minutes per Team to Present

Objectives:
This exercise is designed to get the group to visualize where they are now, where they would like to be and how they can get there. It can be used for corporate direction, new products or specific market developments.

Materials Required:
Pens – Enough colors for each team
Flipchart paper for each group or individual
Blu Tack

Procedure:
Break the group into pairs or groups.

Explain to the group that they are to doodle on one side of the flipchart an island that represents where they are now (the good and bad) with the subject and then on the other side of the flipchart they will draw an island that represents where they would like to be (this is best done on a "landscape" flipchart page, though some use a piece of flipchart paper for each island).

Once the groups have completed or come close to completing the islands, ask them to doodle one or all of the following:

1. A bridge that represents the most direct way for them to get there—on the bridge they can doodle the things, experiences or requirements that they have to get to the other island.
2. There is more than one way to get to their goals—they could represent the journey using boats or airplanes for example.
3. The seas can represent the challenges (rough seas, storms, sea monsters, sharks etc.).

Once you bring the groups back together, allow 3-5 minutes for presentation and discussion per group.

Put the doodles on the wall for the remainder of the session or meeting.

Tips or Discussion Points:

I had one group who had team-building issues that came out really clearly in this exercise. Two different groups represented the journey from one island to the next in very telling ways. One had the entire company swimming across individually (and some sharks eating a few, they were concerned about lay-offs with the new corporate direction), another had each department represented by boats—the best boats were ahead and had the "top brass" on them all the way down to a rickety raft with a department that felt undervalued and under threat by the change. Be prepared for things to surface when doodling is engaged, it is much easier to show how you feel than to voice it. It provided for a whole new conversation and proved to be a very positive way for the group to confront the elephant in the room, we explored it a bit and set it aside as it was not the focus of the session, but we did get down to it in another workshop.

Stereotypes for Strategy

20 minutes for Doodling
3 - 5 minutes for presentation

Objectives:
This exercise is designed to get the group to think about what message they want their product or service to deliver and examine if, as designed or planned, it is viable.

Materials Required:
Pens – Enough colors for each team Flipchart paper for each group or individual Blu Tack

Procedure:
Break the groups out into appropriate groups or pairs.

Explain that they are going create a person to represent a new/existing product or new/existing service. Throw out some stereotypes—would a "nerd" be representative, jock or skater dude? Help them start to think about stereotypes and how they may represent what they're working on.

After 10 minutes of the doodling has passed, then ask them what type of environment this person does best in (doodles needed for a background).

Once you bring the groups back together, allow 3-5 minutes for presentation and discussion per group.

Put the doodles on the wall for the remainder of the session or meeting.

Tips or Discussion Points:

Ask them if the "person" can only survive in the type of environment that they represented—are there alternatives?

Could the product or service have alter egos; appeal to more than one type—how?

What would be the anti-personalities to these people? Who would really "not like" them?

What sort of marketing would appeal to this (or these) groups?

Playing Cards – Product or Market Development

5 - 10 minutes Individual Card Making
10 - 15 minutes for Group Session
3 - 5 minutes for group Presentation & Discussion

Objectives:

When developing a new market or product, there are many different factors to consider. This exercise is designed to allow individuals to write down what they feel are the most important considerations and then to have the group address these issues collaboratively for a clear picture of product and path.

Materials Required:

4 cards for each participant in the group Index Cards (3 x 5) pre-prepared by facilitator (explained in **Tips or Discussion Points**)
Pens – Enough colors for each team Flipchart paper for each group or individual
Flip Chart Paper x 4 for each group
Blu Tack

Procedure:

When the groups arrive, hand them 4 cards each, one of each "suit". Have a flipchart paper or PowerPoint slide explaining what each "suit" represents in the journey of product or market development. (See **Tips or Discussion Points**). You can be economical with your explanation of meanings (depending on the group this can sometimes work best) and only pick a few teaser questions or be explicit and use all of the material in your explanation. Gauge the group and do what suits best.

Ask them to write and issue (doodle to make it clear) key areas specific to the product or market that they feel are the most important for the group to make the project a success. The issue that they state on the card must be relevant to the suit. If you have some people who really have a burning issue that is not represented by the available suit categories, give them a blank card and tell them that they can create the card deck's wild card (or joker).

Gather up the finished cards, shuffle them or throw them into a bucket and mix them up well.

Break them into groups of 3 - 4 and ask each group to select 4 cards each. They are to think about each card and brainstorm on flipchart paper the ways to address the issues raised on each card (it doesn't matter if a group gets all one suit),

Once you bring the groups back together allow 3 - 5 minutes for presentation and discussion per group.

There will be a lot of flipchart papers so it will be impossible (unless you have a really large space) to put them up—you can organize the flipcharts in "Stacks" of suits, staple them and then leave them in the room for people to refer to later on if they'd like to.

Tips or Discussion Points:

I suggest the following 4 areas of discussion for this exercise; if you know of others that are more specific to the group, of course, feel free to make your own! Now's a good time to remind you that if you're doodling these icons on cards, they don't need to be perfect! Just make sure they are consistent on each card.

In the interest of saving preparation time, you can just doodle one of the suit symbols on one side of the cards and ask them to "fill" in the other side with their doodles or thoughts on the challenges/issues. Alternatively, you can make the cards look like "real" playing cards and doodle in the four corners.

Also – REMEMBER – you can doodle whatever symbol you'd like, below are just suggestions!

Technically

Function, what is the purpose of your product or service, are there limits?

Is it designed/or is it designed appropriately?

What about production/delivery issues—can you offer the product or service at a reasonable price?

Society and Legality

Is your product or service subject to any laws or restrictions—do you know?

Legal issues could be: ownership, distribution, operation and restrictions?

What about safety issues?

Will your product or service contribute or degrade any natural resources?

How about quality of life—will your product or service generate a net benefit to society?

Market and the Money

Is your potential share of the market enough for it to be viable?

What degree of price stability is there/do you expect?

Is there enough revenue potential to justify it?

Does the product or service depend on the sale of other products/services?

Would your product or service fade away if others were removed?

Is there development potential for add ons/a family of products/services?

Can your customers easily understand how to use your product or services/what it is/can do?

Does your product or service answer a particular need?

Are the advantages and purpose of your product/service easily apparent?

What is the cost of promoting your product/service? Is it reasonable?

If it's a product, are there easy distribution channels or will they need to be developed?

List the Risks

Are there any alternatives to your product/service? If so, how are clients going to make the choice for yours? Last longer? Look better? Better price?

What stage of development are you at? When you are ready, do you feel it will be "the right time"?

What amount of effort will the market research for your product/service take—how much will be needed to determine price, place and promotion?

Does this require a large investment to develop?

Does it require a large investment to market and launch?

How long will it take to recover the investment? Longer or shorter than the peak demand threshold?

Is there real potential for it to be profitable?

Corporate Culture &
Business Overviews

Multiple Destinations

15 - 20 Minutes Doodling
3 - 5 Minutes Group Presentation

Objectives:
To give the group a way to track where they have come from (as a department or business) and map where they want to go, what the mini-destinations are to the final destination and how they might get there.

Materials Required:
Pens – Enough colors for each team
Flipchart paper for each group
Blu Tack

Procedure:
Break the groups out into groups of 3 - 4.

Share the quote:
"Life is a Journey with Multiple Destinations"

Ask the groups to think about their corporate or department's journey; where they have come from (I usually go back 5 years, sometimes more or less is appropriate) and where they want to arrive in 5 years (remind them that the road of course continues beyond that!).

Each group should now doodle a map that tracks the 10-year period. Remind them that normal mapping can include landmarks, one-way roads, roundabouts, rest stops and a whole host of things. The high and low points of the journey should be noted as well (this can be done by type of road, dirt/paved/highway). It doesn't have to be a doodle-done AA road map; I have had groups map ocean crossings, trips down the Amazon, airline travel (with states representing different processes or experiences), a map of a metropolis type city (with slums and suburbs included), one group did a hiking trail (using different sized and types of mountains and valleys to show experiences). The possibilities are endless.

Once you bring the groups back together allow 3 - 5 minutes for presentation and discussion per group.

Put the flipcharts around the room for the rest of the meeting/session.

Tips or Discussion Points:

If time allows, before the group doodling begins, allow 2 - 3 minutes for each person to doodle while they think about their experiences and where they believe the company or department is heading.

Conquistador or Colonist

20 Minutes to Doodle

2 - 3 Minutes a team to explain/discuss

Objectives:

This simple division of intentions will allow the group to examine what the corporate culture is in dealing with various aspects of an organization. It can open discussions into what is being done well and what (and how) things can be improved.

Materials Required:

Pens – Enough colors for each team

Flipchart paper for each group or individual

Blu Tack

Procedure:

Break the groups out into groups of 3 - 4.

Explain to them that they are going to think about the organization using Conquistadors and Colonist as representatives of their organization.

Historically, Conquistadors were sent around the world, to plunder and take as much as they could get from the land, resources and people that they found. Conversely, Colonists were sent out to live and build new lives and cooperative communities (it has to be said, this is not necessarily an accurate description, but for the purposes of this game, that's the definition).

At this point, let them know that you would like them to think about their organization—put up a flipchart of all or some of the following organizational functions/experiences:

The Way Top Managers Lead

Internal Communications

Departmental Teamwork
Internal Relations between Departments
Flow of Internal information
Flow of Work
Recognition for jobs well done

Ask them to consider if their corporate culture is one of Conquistadors or Colonists with respect to each of the categories listed. Their doodle interpretation of the categories needs to demonstrate which approach is taken for which aspect.
Pull them back together and have the groups present.

Put the flipcharts around the room for the rest of the meeting/session.

Tips or Discussion Points:
The representations can be done in a variety of creative ways—I've had a few very interesting interpretations. One had a group doodle colonists (representing the categories) being attacked by Conquistador categories; another listed/doodled the sorts of things that Conquistadors/Colonists would use and illustrated them using the categories and another interesting one was a doodled Conquistador and Colonist whose body parts represented the different categories.

If there are wildly variant perceptions about how the different categories are handled, ask them why.

If they can see areas where things could shift from Conquistador to Colonist, what are they and how could they move from the Conquistador style to the Colonist style.

Are there any categories that have both Conquistador and Colonist aspects?

What Are We?

5 - 10 Minutes for Doodling
2 - 3 Minutes per Individuals to Present

Objectives:
A quick way to gauge the mood of a group who are about to engage in process review or address tough organizational issues.

Materials Required:
Pens – Enough colors for each person
Blank A4 paper – 1 or 2 sheets for each person
Blu Tack

Procedure:
When you are about to launch into heavy discussions and the general mood of the room is feeling the pressure, ask them to take 3 minutes to draw whatever animal, thing, place, person, random doodle shapes they think could represent the problem at hand. They are to spend some time doodling/thinking about the issues the group are about to tackle (you could put the theme or description of the purpose of the meeting/workshop up for them to refer to).

Ask each person to present their doodle and what it means to them. In some cases (you will have to gauge your group), doing this will hurtle the group back into the trenches, use your intuition (doodle while they are to decide which the best route is!). If you feel it is best to allow them not to present and just contemplate what's been going on, when the time is up just tell them to put them aside and get straight back down to business.

Tips or Discussion Points:
If the mood of the room was edgy, this exercise will help to calm the tensions and allow some space before the heavy work. Alternatively, if you are already in the middle of the process and feel the group is becoming entrenched and progress is at

a standstill, pausing for this exercise can give some space for egos to calm and for perspective on the issues to develop quietly.

This exercise can be viewed as a mini-doodle meditation and doesn't only have to be used in tense situations; if a group is losing its focus (because they're having too much fun), pausing for this can help to bring everybody back to the issue at hand.

The Devil You Know

10 Minutes for Doodling
3 - 4 Minutes per Group to Present

Objectives:
To get your team to recognize problems or obstacles that are thriving within the team or organization.

Materials Required:
Pens – Enough colors for each team
Flipchart paper for each group
Blu Tack

Procedure:
Break the group into groups of 3 - 4.

This can be a great starter to a day's agenda that has some tough decisions about internal processes to make. Explain to them that they are being tasked to identify the areas or departments that are persistently creating obstacles to change or functions of the company. The devils can represent processes, procedures, relationships; whatever they feel needs to be changed.

This is a particularly good exercise just after some changes have been made or when trying to address process re-design. It can also be useful for higher-level management to help to identify problems within or between workgroups.

Have the groups pull back together and present their devils. Allow for whole group discussion as appropriate.

Put the flipcharts around the room for the rest of the meeting/session.

Tips or Discussion Points:

This exercise can help people to view things more objectively by opening discussions and identifying areas that they know are problems, but have just been trying to get around them without addressing them. It can create a space for examining the way things have "always been done" and open avenues of conversation about ways to look at new and more efficient ways of working by dealing with the devils they know more directly.

Transformers

20 - 30 Minutes Doodling
3 - 5 Minutes for Presentations

Objectives:
To get your group to look at where they are now/what they are and where they need to be/what they need to be.

Materials Required:
Pens – Enough colors for each team
Flipchart paper for each group
Blu Tack

Procedure:
Break the group into groups of 3 - 4.

Have the group doodle a transformer vehicle that represents what they are now.

Then the group should explore what the organization or department need to become/be and draw a transformer that represents the changes, adjustments and additions. Remind them that in the blockbuster *Transformer* movies you could still identify elements of what they were in the first stage (in their doodle, this represents the skills/good stuff that they need to carry to the next phase), so elements in the 2nd transformer should have recognizable elements from the 1st transformer doodle.

Have the groups pull back together and present their devils. Allow for whole group discussion as appropriate.

Put the flipcharts around the room for the rest of the meeting/session.

Tips or Discussion Points:

You could adjust this exercise and some groups just doodle the 1st transformer (where they are now/what they are now) and the other groups to design a transformer of where they want to be/what they want to be. If doing this, tell the groups doodling the 2nd transformer to clearly identify what they are bringing along from what they do now in their doodle. The transformers invariably don't come close to looking the same in style; however, you will find areas of agreement of what needs to be carried on from the current to the next phase so it can be useful to identify consensus in the group.

Appendices

A bit of Trainer Banter for "selling the idea of doodling" to your company, a client or during trainings & meetings

I thought it might be a nice idea to offer those of you running these workshops a few random facts and a few fun and interesting facts for use with your doodle exercises. Let's face it, everybody likes a bit of trivia!

Doodle Credibility - In Defence of the Doodle

Doodling is getting on the radars of some pretty credible disciplines; it's actually becoming acceptable for the "serious" sciences to consider. Many fields of study, education (attention holding), psychology (personality trait indicator), psychiatry (mental state indicator), humanities (insights into historical figures and events), and now, even neuroscience (right and left brain activity) are turning an eye to doodling.

In an article published by The Lancet, entitled, "Doodling and the default network of the brain"[1], doodles and doodling can provide insights not only into brain function generally but also into cognitive function.

It may look like doodling is just "kids' stuff", but it seems that there's a whole lot more than meets the eye going on . . .

Benefits of the Doodle
Scientifically speaking . . .

A lot of people think that doodlers aren't paying attention. Let's be honest—who hasn't sat in a meeting and doodled the odd doodle? It's hard to resist. While some may think that scribbling random shapes and pictures while thinking or listening is nothing short of a rude sign that someone isn't listening, quite the opposite is true.

---

[1]   Cite link: doi:10.1016/S0140-6736(08)61345-8

According to Jackie Andrade of the University of Plymouth, doodlers actually remember more than non-doodlers when asked to retain tedious and difficult information. Doodling can actually keep your mind from wandering—quite the opposite of a daydream exercise, doodling demands quite a bit of brain processing, but not the "executive function" kind (which requires projection, planning, comparisons etc.). Doodling requires very little high order thought, it forces your brain to expend just enough energy to stop your head from wandering and daydreaming about that great holiday you'd love to be taking.

Jackie Andrade's research results were published in Applied Cognitive Psychology and she found that subjects given doodling to do not only did better when they were quizzed on what they were listening to while doodling (an excruciatingly painful phone message of random facts information), but they also did 29% better than their non-doodling companions on an impromptu pop-quiz of their general memory given right after their "official experiment" assessment.

One of the largest known objective doodle studies was conducted by W S Maclay, E Guttmann and W Mayer-Gross in 1938, when they studied 9000 doodles sent in by the public in response to a competition run by *The Evening Standard*. The study's results found that doodles were produced during states of idleness, boredom, leisure, meditation and "affective tension"—indecision, concentration, expectation and impatience.

They went on to say that when an individual doodles, the brain tends to be highly creative because it is occupied, for instance, occupied in solving a problem or generating new ideas or designs. So, for some doodlers, doodling may be one of the crucial elements for creativity, while for others, it may simply be a way to relax or entertain themselves while thinking about other things.

The trio also identified a health benefit to doodling; they found that when doodling while bored, stressed, impatient or full of indecision, the act of scribbling and doodling can actually relieve some of those feelings. They did conclude, however, that to analyse the doodles for real meaning or interpretation simply can't hold any real credence as symbols and pictures will mean different things due to experience, culture and simply how each of us interprets the world (but it can be a bit of fun to try).

Brain Doodling

Drawing spontaneously and filling a space with pen ink is engaging your right brain & your left-brain.

The right side of the brain:

Uses feeling

"Big picture," oriented

Imagination rules

Symbols and images

Present and future

Philosophy & religion

Can "get it" (i.e. meaning)

Believes

Appreciates

Spatial perception

Knows object function

Fantasy based

Presents possibilities

Impetuous

Risk taking

Left Brain Doodling is more specific—it's about planning, measuring, ratios.

The left side of the brain:

Uses logic

Detail oriented

Facts rule

Words and language

Present and past

Math and science

Can comprehend

Knowing

Acknowledges

Order/pattern perception
Knows object name
Reality based
Forms strategies
Practical
Safe

So, when you doodle your ideas, information that you "know" or focusing on goals, you're getting the best from both sides!

Doodling for Health

Doodling for Meditation

If you have attempted meditation (and, like me, failed), there is a new field of meditation called the Meditative Doodle. The method is to commit to a quiet 30 minutes or more to the process and, of course, start with a blank page. Find a quiet place and just start doodling. This will shut down (or keep busy) the chatting side of your mind and is a "bona fide" way of achieving the same state of being that traditional meditative techniques can achieve. Including some form of meditation in your life has many well-documented benefits such as improved physical health, increased mental sharpness and an increased ability to deal with our emotions in a healthy way.

Doodling in Illness

The City of Hope National Cancer Center in Los Angeles runs a programme started by Carol Edmonton called "Create While You Wait". She is a two time survivor of breast cancer and discovered while she was ill that doodling was one way that helped her deal with the incredible challenge of facing such a serious illness. The programme offers patients and family members a creative outlet while waiting for treatment and/or doctors' appointments. Her programme is also now being run at the Christie Cancer Centre in Manchester, England. Carol is a trained physical therapist and has published two books, "Create While You Wait . . . a doodle book for all ages" and "Connections . . . the Sacred Journey between two Points". If you would like to find out more about her work, you can find her at http://www.sacreddoodles.com/.

Jungian Mandala Meditation

Carl Jung describes Mandalas as "the psychological expression of the totality of the self". He believed a person could find the seed-center of themselves through the drawing of personal mandalas. For Jung, the center point of the mandala represented your core self and all of the elements beyond represented the extraneous elements of your environment and psyche. Within the personal mandala he would discern the internal elements (ideas, emotions, compulsions) as well as the external elements (relationships, environment) all of which interface to make up the person. Jung believed that within a mandala's shapes, patters and elements we can discover the sacred matrix of ourselves and our part of the cosmos or universe.

Mandalas can be found in many cultures, faiths, traditions and mythologies. The most notable mandala practices can be found in Buddhism and Hinduism. However, for these faiths, the mandala is viewed differently from Jung's interpretation. In Buddhist mandala meditations, the mandala functions as a way to deconstruct self-centeredness, which culminates in the existential act of dissolving the elaborate self-constructions into emptiness.

Some Famous Compulsive Doodlers:

Most Presidents2 of the United States, to name a few

George Washington (geometric shapes mostly)

Thomas Jefferson

John F. Kennedy (compulsive yacht doodler)

Ronald Reagan (believe it or not, he liked to draw cowboys and football players)

Bill Clinton (at the time of this writing, his private presidential papers aren't public yet)

Barack Obama (he offered an Official Doodle for "national Doodle Day" during his first term as President)

Poets & Authors:

Ralph Waldo Emerson (his Harvard compositions are covered with doodles of people, fish and scrolls)

Samuel Beckett

Sylvia Plath

Vladimir Nabokov

Fyodor Dostoyevsky

Kurt Vonnegut

Mark Twain

Mathematicians & Scientists

Stanislaw Ulam, doodling during a mathematics lecture came up with the perfect doodle to explain prime numbers (the Ulam spiral)

Sir Martin Rees, Astronomer Royal and Master of Trinity College doodled part of the Universe and donated it to a charity auction.

---

2   *If presidential doodles really interest you, pick up the book called Presidential Doodles: Two Centuries of Scribbles, Scratches, Squiggles and Scrawls from the Oval Office (David Greenberg and Cabinet Magazine). More information on the George H. W. Bush doodle can be found there too.*

Artists
Michelangelo left behind hundreds of scribbled images (on one is written, "must get round to painting the ceiling")

Leonardo Da Vinci's doodles and drawings proved inspirational—his scribbles foresaw the helicopter and hydraulic pump for example)

A Few Other Famous People
Bill Gates. Bill Gates famously left a page of doodles on Tony Blair's desk after an Economic summit held in Davos (2005). International psychologist and handwriting experts had a field day analysing what they meant.

Hilary Clinton. Her doodles on speech notes during a UN Security Council meeting in 2012 were deemed so newsworthy that The Daily Mail published an article analysing the series of interlocked circles and stars.

Winston Churchill. He was fond of drawing 3D boxes and spirals.

Vidal Sassoon, drawer of triangles and planets.

The Doodle Down the Ages

Well, if you're asking me, and I think it's a safe bet that if you're reading this you might want to know what I think, doodling has been around at least since the oldest cave paintings—that would be since the Aurignacian period (about 40,000 years ago).

Around 3200 B.C. pictographic record keeping in clay began in Mesopotamian society. Pictures were drawn in clay to convey information and some of the tablets that have been found have included random decorated edges and images on the margins of the dried clay pieces.

Moving considerably forward, the medieval monks called doodles "probation pennae" (proving of the pen). Doodling seems to be an integral part of human nature, there are medieval manuscripts that have margins covered in scribes' names written over and over or the same spiral patters repeated in random order and margins.

It seems intuitive expression through doodling has been an integral theme for humankind as long as we've been on earth.

Before the 20th century doodle wasn't actually about drawing; the closest term in English was scribble (but, of course, scribbling is not doodling).

Prior to the 20th century, the term doodle wasn't actually about drawing at all; it was a way to describe someone who was idle. Linguistic historians think that, initially, the Portuguese word for foolish (doudo) and the low German word for foolish (dudel) amalgamated to the Samuel Johnson Dictionary definition of doodle as "a trifler, an idler" (published first in 1755).

Doodle as we know the term nowadays, seems to have come from Mr. Russell M. Arundel who wrote a book called "Everybody's Pixillated" (1937). He defined doodles as " . . . a scribble or sketch made while the conscious mind is concerned with matters wholly unrelated to the scribbling."

In his writing, he put forward the idea that a developed or, civilized, man's natural state was one of "pixilation", an enchanted state that was pixie-like and buried beneath the cloak of business and modern life's cares. He believed that doodling could help us revel the pixieness that we all possess no matter how far buried by the worries and woes of modern living. In defending his point of doodling as a way to tap into what I believe we could now call intention and intuition, Mr. Arundel used examples of mid-century leaders like Franklin Delano Roosevelt and Cab Galloway; saying that they used doodling as a sort of meditation to get to the core of decisions and situations.

The idea of doodling took off from there (if only with a relatively short burst of attention). Even W H Auden wrote a poem about man's search for meaning, substance and identity in an ever-changing industrialised world. He seems to have been aware of the Arundel's idea; in his work "The Age of Anxiety" published in 1948, he describes

" . . . Moulds and monsters on memories stuffed
With dead men's doodles, dossiers written
In lost lingos, too long an account
To take out in trade, no time either . . ."

There is a strong argument that most of us are now on the same search in response to our hyper-developing totally distracting technological world and that perhaps doodling can help people and their organisations plug into what seems to be missing from a lot of our modern times—connection . . .

Some Random Doodle Thoughts

A Picture is Worth A Thousand Words . . .

This common English "throw away" phrase demonstrates our inherent recognition that the visual medium is perhaps more powerful than the literary.

Take Facebook, for example; presuming you are on Facebook already, it's a safe bet your friends or you have posted quotes that include a background photo to help to pass along the message of the words. You find similar messages on posters, in magazines and inspirational quote books. The images convey messages beyond the limitations of language.

The press and media are fully aware that photos have a unique ability to elicit a visceral reaction in a way that words can rarely do (though there are some notable poetic exceptions).

Shocking and sometimes manipulated convincing photographs covering world news can sway global opinions far more than the most well written articles because pictures are immediate and instantly convey messages. Cartoonists would also be aware of the power images have over words.

It seems we all have a collective understanding of the power of communicating visually, but in the running of day to day business we still have a need to hang on to the words as our only means of communicating and connecting with our staff and clients (it even happens in businesses all about advertising/marketing—often they do a brilliant job for clients, but forget the same creative message methods offered with visual medium can work internally too).

Yankee Doodle Dandy

Now the date of Johnson's Dictionary (1755) is of particular relevance to me (see the section entitled "The Doodle Down the Ages") as I'm from the United States. Johnson's definition of doodle was picked up by the British and Hessian soldiers who called American revolutionaries "Yankee Doodles"; who doesn't know that song? It's actually sung patriotically now and is even the state anthem of Connecticut! Incredible as the song is, it isn't exactly complimentary to your average American. Then again, I did grow up singing it and, of course, know all the words.

I just hope that when we took it on as a "National song" of sorts, it was with a bit of irony (though, sadly, perhaps not).

Some Really Random Doodle-bug Facts . . . in case you been wondering about them . . .

Antlions (nicknamed doodle-bugs) are a type of woodlice larvae. In an attempt to briefly raise the tone, the doodlebug's Latin name is Myrmeleo). Seeing as I am familiar with doodlebugs, we'll stick with doodlebug from here on out.

Apparently, they got their nickname in North America because of the odd winding spirals that they leave in the sand while building their pits—they look like random doodles of course.

In the southern states of America kids are taught a song to sing (though it is often really just shouted) at the hole to make the doodlebug come out. Similar stuff happens in Africa, the Caribbean, China and Australia.

I can easily recall many spring days singing this rhyme down a doodlebug hole:

Doodlebug, doodlebug,
Come out of your hole;
Your house is on fire
And your children will burn

Clearly there wasn't a lot for a kid to do in rural Virginia . . . however it must have been a timeless southern child's task. Even Mark Twain must have done it—in *Tom Sawyer* the doodlebug is called on to find Tom's lost marbles (the meaning of that can be taken more than one way I reckon . . .).

In World War II, the German V-1 Flying bomb was referred to as a Doodlebug because of the buzzing noise it made.

Later still, the doodlebug rears its popular culture head; Apollo 16 astronaut Charles Duke compared some of the lunar craters to doodle-bug pits. A transcript of his lunar conversations even includes his own version of the childhood doodle-bug song, he sings Doodlebug, Doodle-bug, are you at home?" Pretty funny, huh?

Rather bizarrely, doodle-bug is also a term of endearment in the South, I've even caught myself calling my own children it on occasion . . . On reflection it seems a strange endearment, as essentially it seems I am calling them woodlice larvae . . .

Google Doodles

In 1998, when the founders of Google were starting, they recognized the "power of the doodle". The story goes, they played around with the logo the first time when they attended the party of the globe, Burning Man (in the Nevada desert); they put a stick man behind the 2nd "o" to indicate that they were heading to the party. The doodling seems to have taken it from there, with more ideas and meanings communicated through playing with the logo.

It's taken off to such an extent that they even have a Doodle Department with a team of illustrators (called Doodlers) to keep up with the ideas, events and messages that Google wants to send with their logo.

Google even encourages input from anyone on the globe—all you have to do is doodle and send doodle ideas along to their team.

If you're an aspiring Google Doodler, here's the email: proposals@google.com

Snicker doodles

A snicker doodle is a butter based cookie that is flavored with cinnamon, made in the United States. They most likely came from Germany originally where there is a cookie with similar butter dough called the schneckennudeln (which means snail noodles) and the name evolved to something a bit more "American" sounding.

doodlevision Business and Group Services

Doodlevision Business Services:

Mission, Vision & Values Connection, Re-Connection and Creation –
Creating a Clear Message

Getting the Message Out
Corporate Communication Strategies (Interior and Client Relations)
What your organisational aim is (MISSION OR PURPOSE)
Where the organisation is headed (VISION FOR THE FUTURE)
Why the organisation does what it does (VALUES – WHY)

Brainstorming Sessions
New Products and Services, Business Strategies, Sustainability Challenges &
Marketing Strategies

Management & Leadership Strategies
Whole Organisations & Departments

Addressing Business Specific Challenges
Solution Focused + Problem Focused Approaches = Best Strategy

Team Building and Getting To Know
Sessions for Boards, management, Leaders and Staff

Getting to know you, your needs and requirements
Cross Sessions with Clients/Target Groups and Organisations. A creative way to
conduct market research, customer satisfaction and develop strong relationships

Organisational Assessment – Does everyone in your organisation understand:

What your organisational aim is? (MISSION OR PURPOSE)
Where the organisation is headed? (VISION FOR THE FUTURE
Why the organisation does what it does? (VALUES – WHY)

AND . . . .

DOODLE ASSISTED CONFERENCE NOTES – Everyone is looking to do something a little bit special and innovated when organising a conference or seminar—our Graphic Illustrator will stand on stage and doodle notes for your conference attendees, so they can randomly doodle while they listen (and remember more)! The notes will be made available to all participants via email at the end of the sessions—the visual representation of the speakers and conference content will ensure that your organisation Connects, Re Connects & Creates a new and innovative way to get your message across!

Why not Consider doodlevision

The **doodlevision** Way will help you and your group par down to core meaning and message in an engaging and fun way. How many of us have sat in meetings where people get tangled up in language to such a degree that by the time you walk out, you're less clear about the issues and strategies than when you walked in?

Who hasn't walked out of a long meeting or workshop intended to motivate and clarify with less purpose, understanding and passion?

The **doodlevision** Way is not just about getting back to the core meaning—it's about putting the fun and passion back into you and your organisation.

Doodlevision is about losing all the words and getting back to the point of it all – the big (and little) PICTURE – dump the complicated statements, convoluted messages, matrices and spreadsheets and give everyone what is needed now more than ever, a bit of **doodlevision.**

Time to give your educated, terribly clever and wide-vocabulary mind a bit of a holiday . . . Lay down your keyboard, smart phone, tablet and submit your self to a new way of creating and understanding.

From here on out it's going to be about the way of the marker, the way of the magic marker . . . .